BY THE EDITORS OF CONSUMER GUIDE®

HARMONICA
Playing Made Easy

A Complete Step-by-Step
Instruction Book for the Beginner

PUBLICATIONS INTERNATIONAL, LTD.

Louis Weber, C.E.O.
Publications International, Ltd.
7373 North Cicero Avenue
Lincolnwood, Illinois 60646

ISBN 0-7853-0745-1

Contributing Writer:
Dan Landt

Dan "Skip" Landt has studied harmonica with some of America's finest harmonica players, including Don Less of The Harmonicats, Sugar Blue, and Peter "Madcat" Ruth, and his own harmonica playing has been heard on television documentaries and commercials. Since 1985, he has taught introductory and intermediate harmonica to more than 1,000 students at the Old Town School of Folk Music, Chicago, America's first permanent school for the study of folk music and folk instruments, founded in 1957.

Illustrations: Lauren Shavell, Leonid Mysahov

The Arrow Method is used by permission of Hohner, Inc.

CONTENTS

INTRODUCTION:
Music in Your Pocket

Making music in your own home can be a pleasure. But for harmonica players, the real pleasure is carrying their source of homemade musical fun with them throughout the day, wherever they go. So, let's get you on your way to a lifetime of "music in your pocket."

The harmonica is probably the easiest instrument for a beginner. The holes are ingeniously arranged. For many of the songs in this book, most of the notes you need to play are right next to each other. After you've mastered the simple beginner's skills shown in this book, a whole world of music will be open to you. Be sure to read and work on these beginner's skills first; they're the key to moving ahead. Learning and practicing single notes, moving between notes, and sustaining notes will give you a solid platform for your playing.

Once that platform is built—once you have those skills—go ahead and experiment! Try picking out melodies by trial and error. Also, don't feel restrained to playing songs exactly as they are written; in some cases, the songs in this book have been simplified. Your skills platform is a launching pad. When you are ready, just take off! Now, let's get started.

Holding the Harmonica

Hold the harmonica in your left hand (your right hand if you're left-handed), between your thumb and index finger. It should nestle comfortably there. Hold it toward the back so that there's plenty of room for your lips to wrap around the holes. The numbers on the harmonica should face upward so you can read them. The low notes (holes 1, 2, and 3) should be in the area to the left of your thumb's knuckle.

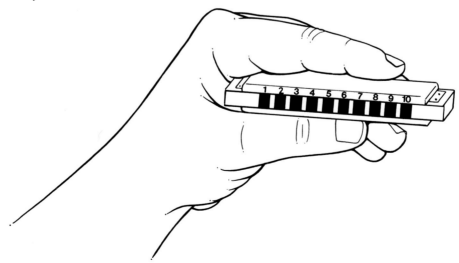

The Holes on Your Harmonica

Examine your harmonica; there are ten holes. Each hole makes two notes: one if you "blow" (blow air out) and one if you "draw" (suck air in). Since you have a harmonica in the key of C, the notes you will find are all in that key.

	1	2	3	4	5	6	7	8	9	10
Blow note	C	E	G	C	E	G	C	E	G	C
Draw notes	D	G	B	D	F	A	B	D	F	A

To keep things very simple, most of the songs in this book will be played with holes 4 through 9. Even without the lower notes, there's plenty of music to play and enjoy. You are also free to experiment with "picking out" melodies by trial and error; it's excellent practice!

Below is the C scale from the 4 hole in standard musical notation with the names of the notes and the hole numbers. The number indicates the hole. An arrow pointed up ↑ means "blow" on that hole; an arrow pointed ↓ down means "draw." A long up ↑ arrow or ↓ down arrow under a hole number means you should hold that note longer.

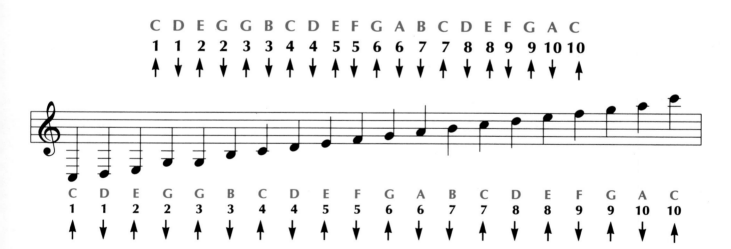

In the middle of your harmonica—holes 4 through 7—is the full "do re mi" scale you've heard about. There's a partial scale on holes 1 to 3 and an almost full scale on holes 7 to 10. We're telling you this so that if you decide to learn melodies by ear, you will find most of the notes you need in the middle and top of your harmonica.

Blowing and Drawing

Playing the harmonica should feel natural, like breathing. So when you "blow," you shouldn't blow as if you were trying to put out a candle—that's far too much air. Try holding the harmonica with your teeth only. Now breathe in and out just as you normally would, but through the harmonica. That's how much air you need. That's also the way you should bring air through the instrument: gently, so that the reeds have plenty of room to sound the note.

When you are playing, control the air flow through the back of your throat. You should direct air into the holes as if you were saying "ah."

Playing Single Notes

Most songs in this book are played with single notes, blowing or drawing one hole at a time. Using the method taught here, single notes are easy. Some people get clear single notes immediately. But for anyone, it shouldn't take long if you follow the steps below.

Without the harmonica, try pushing your lips out as if you were reaching to drink through a straw or as if you were shaping your mouth to whistle. Now look in the mirror. There should be a circular, straw-sized opening that looks like this:

Now, wet your lips and do this again. Press the harmonica to your lips so that the opening in your lips meets the harmonica around the middle (the 4, 5, or 6 hole). The harmonica should be softly nestled to the moist, wet part of your lips. Try to target the 4 hole. Now blow lightly. If you have more than one note, just pucker a bit more. Bingo!

6

Testing Yourself

You shouldn't hear any air escaping around your lips. If you do, the harmonica isn't deeply enough in your mouth. Your lips should be wrapped around the side of the harmonica that has the holes on it, with the soft inner part of your lips making a seal on the hole.

If you are still not certain you have a clear single note, try this other method. Hold the harmonica in two hands. Use your thumbs to cover the unneeded holes. Use your right thumb to cover holes 5 through 10 and your left thumb to cover holes 1 through 3. *Make sure that the 3 and 5 holes are entirely covered.* This leaves the 4 hole uncovered.

Blow into the 4 hole this way first, while blocking the other holes. Then take away your thumbs and try playing using only your lips. Blowing the harmonica should give you the 4 hole (C) very clearly. If you're still not sure you have a single, clear note, use a tape recorder to tape yourself playing the note both ways.

You may need to make some adjustments. Try wetting your lips. Try pushing the harmonica more deeply into your lips or puckering more. Sometimes just relaxing helps; your teeth should be slightly apart.

Reading Music

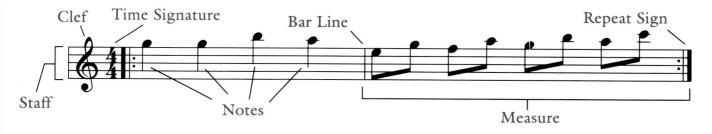

Staff: The staff is the name used to describe the five horizontal parallel lines.
Clef: The clef is a universal symbol for music. The treble clef is shown here.
Notes: The notes are the individual components of a melody.
Bar lines: The bar lines are the vertical lines that divide the staff into sections called measures.
Measures: When you look at a line of music, a measure is the space between the bar lines.
Time signature: The time signature tells you how many beats are in each measure.
Repeat signs: Repeat signs tell you to repeat a section of measures. When you approach a repeat sign on the left side of a bar line, go back in the music to where repeat signs appear on the right side of a bar line and play from there.

Understanding Rhythm

The songs in this book use four time signatures: 4/4, 3/4, 6/8, and 2/4; most are in either 3/4 or 4/4 time. The top number tells the number of beats per measure; the bottom number tells you the value of the note that has one beat. So, 4/4 time has four quarter-note beats per measure; 6/8 time has six eighth-note beats per measure. But what do these notes look like?

Eighth notes **Quarter note** **Half note** **Whole note**

How to Learn Quickly

The above quick introduction is for people who don't yet read music. But you don't need to read music to enjoy these songs. Whether or not you read music, try some of the following tips:

• Work first on a familiar song. For the first few songs, follow the instructions.
• Practice the highlighted skills before trying the song.
• In general, keep to the order the songs appear in the book when getting started.

but...

• Feel free to jump to the children's songs at the back of the book.
• After you've picked up the skills, play for fun. The harmonica is ideal for experimenting. Let your whim be your guide!

A line of music may also include rests where there is silence for the duration designated by the time value of the rest.

Eighth rest **Quarter rest** **Half rest** **Whole rest**

A note with a dot next to it gets time and a half. For example, a dotted quarter note gets the time value of the quarter note plus an eighth note.

Dotted quarter note **Dotted half note**

Advancing Your Playing

Many people can enjoy years of harmonica playing using the skills and songs shown in this book. Others will want to try something new. There are other types of music you will be able to play using the skills you learn here (and some harmonicas in different keys):

Hymns: Traditional hymns are excellent for harmonica playing. Many have simple melodies, not much harder than those you find here.

Popular/folk country songs: Many standards from long ago to the mid-20th century will sound very good on your harmonica.

Fiddle tunes: These catchy melodies using lots of notes usually do not have words. Going between blow and draw notes on different holes is the key here.

Irish music: Much Irish music, usually played on a penny-whistle, concertina, or fiddle, can be adapted for harmonica after you are able to move quickly from note to note.

Chug-style playing: A very rhythmic style, using chords. To try this out, draw in smoothly on the 1, 2, and 3 holes at once. Try a pattern, such as draw-draw-blow, draw-draw-blow.

Simple blues: Many early and simple blues songs can be played with the basic skills you'll learn in this book.

You can also add a new musical dimension of "get down" blues and jazz playing. The skills required here are greater. One technique involves "bending" notes.* This technique lets you achieve notes not otherwise available on the harmonica.

To try "bending," practice saying "eee-yew." Try to say it using just your tongue and without moving your lips. Now, without the harmonica, draw in while saying "eee-yew." Now take the harmonica and gently draw in on the 4 hole; make a long constant tone and hold it as long as possible. Try this again, but shortly after starting to draw, make that "eee-yew" sound. The note should "bend" down at least a bit. By working on this, you should be able to get the 4 draw (D) to go down, perhaps to C sharp. Work on this and you'll be making a start toward playing the blues.

Note bending is used when playing songs written in keys that your harmonica is not pitched in. For example, you would bend a G to F sharp when playing a song written in G if your harmonica is pitched in C.

CHAPTER 1
Playing Single Notes

As you've seen, playing clear single notes isn't difficult. But this skill needs development. The songs in this section were chosen to give you step-by-step practice playing single notes. The songs reflect different combinations and patterns of blow and draw notes. If you play these songs **slowly and clearly**, you'll be well on your way to mastering the most important beginner's skill. Each song is introduced by a note stating your **objective**, followed by information on **what to practice** *before* trying the song itself. Song notes also include a **tip** that will be helpful in your **playing** of the song. If you are not familiar with a particular song, move on to the next one. Playing music is easiest if you are guided *both* by what you see on the page *and* by your own previous knowledge of the song.

SKIP TO MY LOU

Objective: Clear single notes while moving from blow to draw on different holes. Emphases: 6 blow to 4 draw, 5 blow to 4 draw.

Before playing the entire song:
Practice blowing the 6 hole, then sliding down and drawing the 4 hole.
Practice blowing the 5 hole, then drawing the 4 hole.

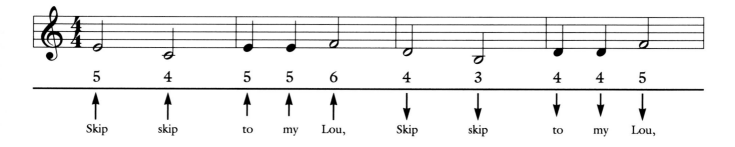

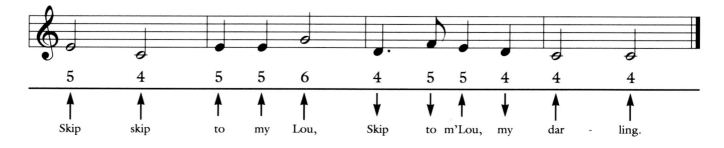

CRIPPLE CREEK (VERSE)

Objective:	Clear single notes while moving from blow hole to blow hole, from draw hole to draw hole, and when shifting from blow to draw on the same hole. Emphasis: holes 5, 6, and 7.
Before playing the entire song:	
	Try blowing the 7 hole. If it is not a clear single note, try puckering more and getting your lips more around the harmonica. You may also be using too much air: Blow lightly, as if you were blowing a bubble. Now try getting a clear note blowing the 6, 5, and 4 holes. Try a blow 5, then a draw 5. If both are clear notes, you're ready to go! If you're having some trouble, try the next song, which may be easier for you.
Tip:	To move from hole to hole, *slide*. Keep the harmonica lightly pressed into your lips. If you don't know which hole you're on, stop playing and move to the bottom (left side) of the harmonica; blow each hole, counting as you go. The chorus for this song can be found on page 44.

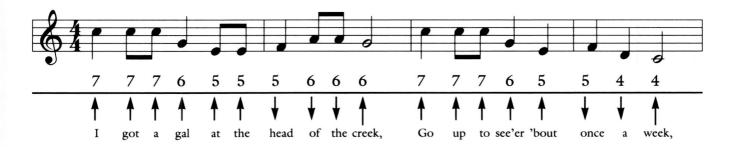

7 7 7 6 5 5 5 6 6 6   7 7 7 6 5 5 4 4

I got a gal at the head of the creek, Go up to see'er 'bout once a week,

7 7 7 6 5 5 5 5 6 6   7 7 7 6 5 5 5 4 4 4

Kisses on the mouth just as sweet as any wine, Wraps her arms 'round me like sweet 'ta-ter vine.

JINGLE BELLS

Objective:	Clear single notes when moving from draw to blow on different holes. Emphases: 4 draw to 5 blow, 4 draw to 6 blow.
Before playing the entire song:	
	Practice these shifts until you can do them well.
Tip:	"Jingle Bells" is one of the many harmonica songs that can be played on two or even three holes. To try this, play the hole shown *and* the hole below it. (That is, begin the song by blowing *both* the 5 hole and the 4 hole.) Whenever the two notes together sound "off," go back to playing only the one shown.

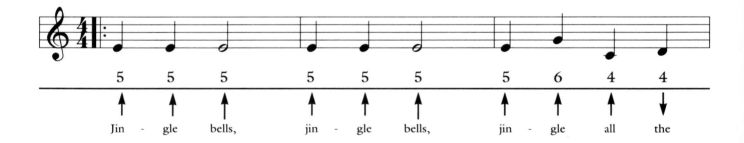

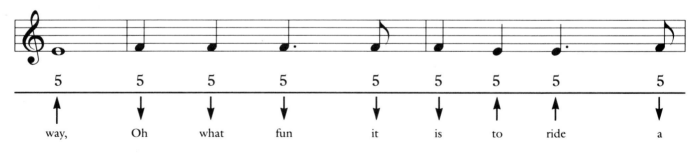

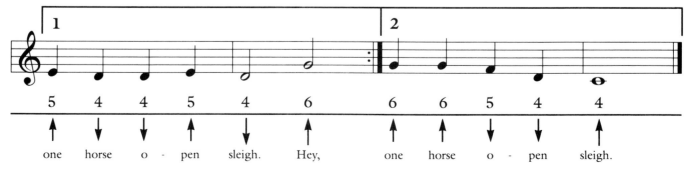

THE CAMPTOWN RACES

by Stephen Foster

Objective: Clear single notes when moving from blow to draw on different holes. Emphasis: 7 blow to 6 draw.

Before playing the entire song:
Practice this shift. You may also want to practice the 5 blow to 4 draw shift again. It came up in "Skip to My Lou"; here you need it for the "doo dahs."

Tip: This is an easy song to play, but don't speed up too much. Even on the long sequences of blow notes (for example, "Goin' to run all night"), each note should be distinct.

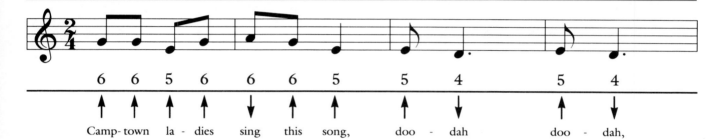

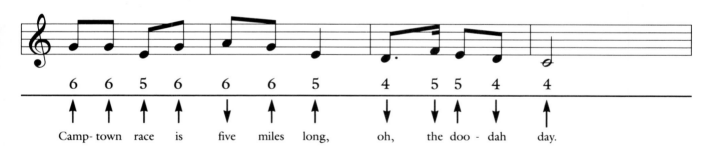

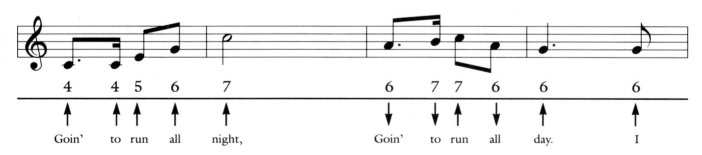

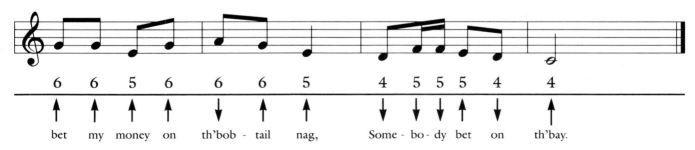

GOOD NIGHT, LADIES

Objective:	Clear single notes when moving from draw to blow on different holes. Emphasis: 4 draw to 5 blow.
Before playing the entire song:	
	Practice this shift, moving cleanly between holes 4 and 5, until it is second nature to you.
Tip:	Notice the long two-beat notes in this song. Be sure to hold these so the notes flow.

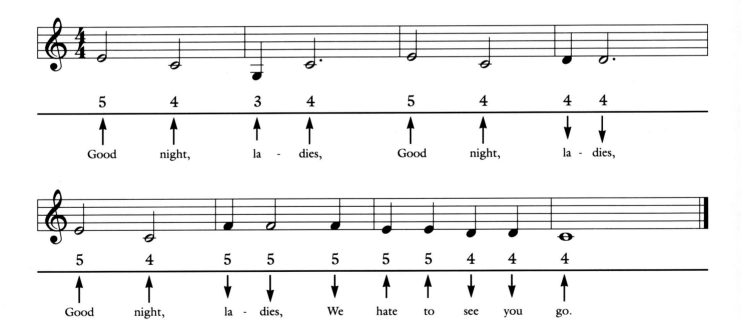

AUNT RHODY

Objective:	Clear single notes when moving from blow to draw on different holes. Emphases: 5 blow to 4 draw, 6 blow to 5 draw.
Before playing the entire song:	Practice these shifts.
Tip:	Also practice the notes in the last phrase "The old grey goose is dead"; the shift from 5 blow to 4 draw should be just as smooth as the movement between the other notes.

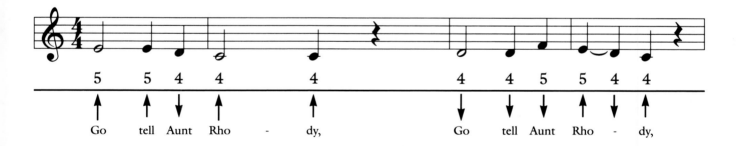

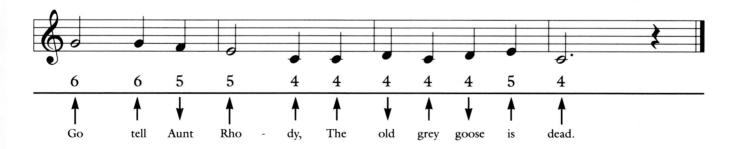

ROW YOUR BOAT

Objective:	Clear single notes when moving from draw to blow and blow to draw. Emphases: 5 draw to 6 blow, 6 blow to 5 draw.
Before playing the entire song:	Practice these shifts.
Tip:	To play this song as a round, have a friend start the song again when you begin the second or third measure.

by E.O. Lyte

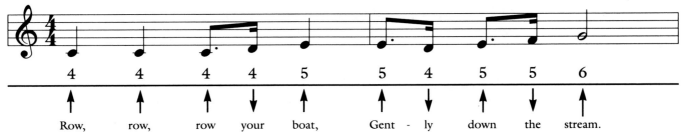

4	4	4	4	5	5	4	5	5	6
↑	↑	↑	↓	↑	↑	↓	↑	↓	↑

Row, row, row your boat, Gent - ly down the stream.

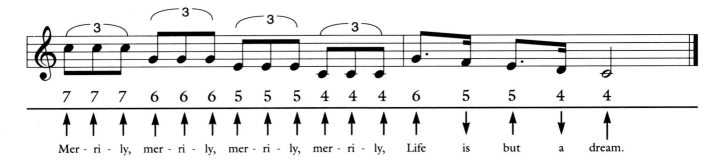

7	7	7	6	6	6	5	5	5	4	4	4	6	5	5	4	4
↑	↑	↑	↑	↑	↑	↑	↑	↑	↑	↑	↑	↑	↓	↑	↓	↑

Mer - ri - ly, mer - ri - ly, mer - ri - ly, mer - ri - ly, Life is but a dream.

KOOKABURRA

Objective:	Clear single notes when moving from blow to draw and draw to blow. Emphases: 7 blow to 6 draw, 5 draw to 6 blow.
Before playing the entire song:	Practice these shifts.
Tip:	When playing the same note several times in quick succession, keep the air flowing through the hole as if you were making a sound like "uh-uh-uh-uh." The air flow is never entirely interrupted.

by Marion Sinclair

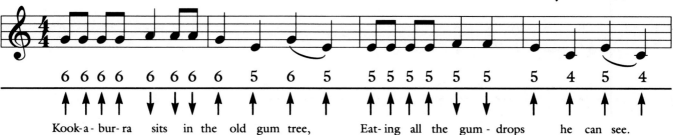

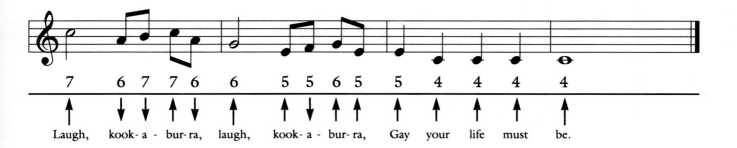

THE COLORADO TRAIL

Objective: Clear single notes when moving from draw to blow and back. Emphasis: 6 draw to 7 blow and back to 6 draw.

Before playing the entire song:
Practice this shift.

Tip: This is an especially soft and tender song that should be played with feeling.

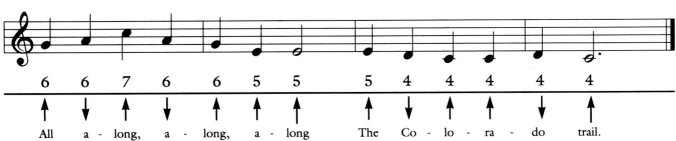

18

CHAPTER 2
Hold That Note

Now that you're playing clear single notes, it's time to learn the next skill, which is *sustaining,* or *holding,* those notes. Much of what we enjoy in music is its flow. In most music, each note flows into the next note to form a connected melody. When you played "Jingle Bells" in the last section, did you play it with a pause after each word, or did each note flow from the last one? The second way—flowing from note to note—is what you should aim for.

To produce this flow is not hard. When playing "Jingle Bells," use your breath continuously. A tad of air should always be moving across the harmonica's reeds. When you move from note to note, slide your lips from hole to hole.

Some notes—such as half notes or whole notes—are specifically marked for holding. For the harmonica, these are shown with a long arrow. This means you should extend those notes for a longer time than others. Ideally, these longer notes will taper off gradually.

Tone

One remarkable fact about the harmonica pertains to tone. People playing the same model of harmonica can sound entirely different. One person can produce a pleasant, open sound; another a controlled, sweet sound; and yet a third, a full, resonant sound.

What's the reason? While the harmonica makes the music, it depends on the individual player to provide the tone. Good tone can give a fascinating quality to your musical notes, so it is worth some effort to learn how to achieve tone.

There are at least five kinds of tone, each of which can be shaped, or modified.

Mouth tone: This is the normal tone you get as a beginner. To vary mouth tone, experiment with how much space you leave between your tongue and your lips. Leaving just a little space will produce a kind of honky-tonk sound; more space will give a more folksy sound.

Hand tone: This tone is produced by using two hands when playing. The left hand holds the harmonica while the right hand "cups" behind it. Cup your hands so tightly that little air can get in or out: Your hands control the flow of air and thus control the tone.

Tongue tone: Vibrato can also be produced with your tongue. While playing a long note, move your tongue rapidly back and forth inside your mouth, either from side to side or up and down.

Throat tone: This tone comes from the very back of your throat. By narrowing and controlling the air flow from here, you can achieve exceptionally good tone.

Diaphragm tone: Singers know their voice must be projected from their diaphragm. This is also true for harmonica players. Practice breathing in and out from your diaphragm (stomach area). If you can play your notes from "way down," you will vastly improve your tone.

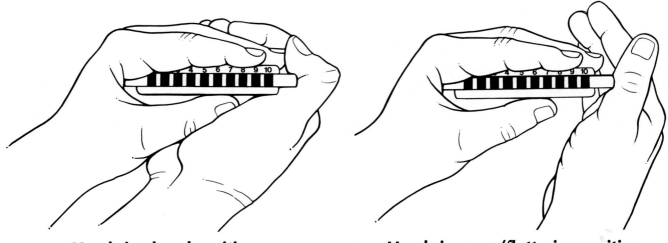

Hands in closed position   **Hands in open/fluttering position**

A way to alter tone is to use your hands for fluttering. To achieve this, "flutter" (move back and forth) your hand behind the harmonica as you play a note, giving a vibrato to your tone.

MICHAEL ROW THE BOAT ASHORE

Objective: Sustaining tones, both on a single note and when moving between notes. Emphases: 6 draw to 6 blow, 5 blow to 4 draw to 4 blow.

Before playing the entire song:
Do a long, gentle blow on the 6 hole; then shift to a long, gentle draw on the 6 hole, with a smooth movement between these. Now try to attain that same smoothness while playing the last three notes of the song: 5 blow, 4 draw, and 4 blow.

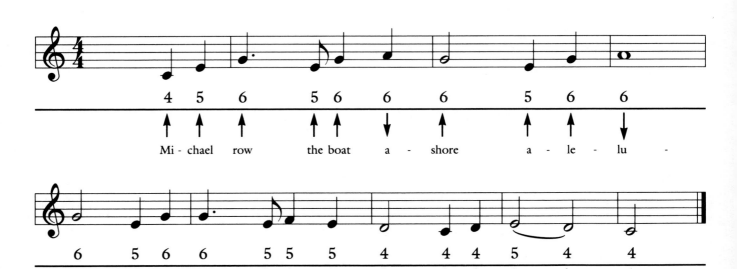

SILENT NIGHT

Objective: Sustaining tones, both on a single note and when moving between notes. Emphases: 5 blow to 8 draw, 6 blow to 5 draw.

Before playing the entire song: Practice starting on the 5 blow and moving up to the 8 draw. After you have that interval down, do a long, gentle blow on the 5 hole followed by a long, gentle draw on the 8 hole.

Tip: This song reaches up to the 8 draw and the 9 draw. The reeds that sound the notes up there are very tiny and can easily be "choked" with too much air. Make a point of using *very little air* when drawing.

SHENANDOAH

Objective:	Sustaining tones, both on a single note and when moving between notes. Emphases: 7 draw to 6 blow, 4 blow to 6 draw to 5 blow.
Before playing the entire song:	Practice these patterns.
Tip:	This song should be played slowly, with long sustained tones after the words "Shenandoah," "you," "river," and "Missouri." In addition to sustaining these notes, you may want to try giving them some extra tone by hand, throat, or diaphragm; see page 19.

Brahms' Lullaby

Objective:	Sustaining tones, both on a single note and when moving between notes. Emphases: 6 blow to 7 draw, 5 blow to 7 blow, 7 blow to 6 draw.
Before playing the entire song:	Practice these patterns.
Tip:	Remember, this is a lullaby. Play it very slowly and try to add tone with your hands, tongue, or diaphragm.

by Johannes Brahms

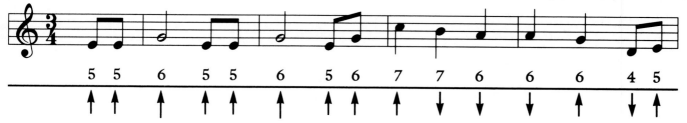

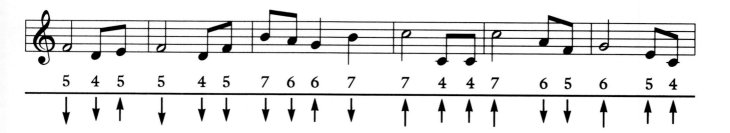

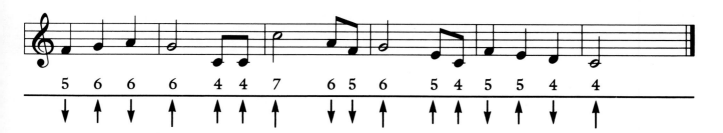

CHAPTER 3
Let the Music Flow

The songs in this section span a range of popular favorites: from cowboy ballads to music hall songs to spirituals. Each calls upon the skills you have learned and provides opportunities to try them in new situations.

This is also the time for you to think beyond the clear notes and the long notes. As you become more comfortable with your harmonica, sequences of notes should begin to come more easily so you can let the music flow!

CLEMENTINE

Objective: Playing at a steady pace, with no hesitation at changes from blow to draw on different holes. Emphases: 6 blow to 5 draw, 5 blow to 4 draw, 4 draw to 3 blow.

Before playing the entire song:
Practice the notes for the phrase, "Oh my darlin' Clementine," which ends with 6 blow to 5 draw to 5 blow to 4 draw. Practice the notes for the phrase, "Dreadful sorry," which ends with 4 draw to 3 blow.

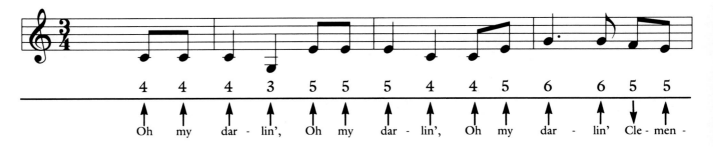

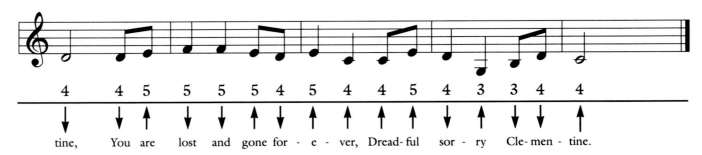

OLD ABE LINCOLN
(THE OLD GRAY MARE)

Objective:	Playing at a steady pace, with no hesitation at changes from blow to draw on different holes. Emphasis: 5 blow to 4 draw.
Before playing the entire song:	
	Practice notes for the phrase, "out of the wilderness," which ends with a 5 blow, 4 draw, 4 blow pattern.
Tip:	When you first play this song, start with the 4 blow on the word "old." When you're comfortable playing it that way, try playing it as it is written here, starting with the 3 blow. Playing these notes in quick succession ("wellold") is a good way to begin this song with a bang!

25

RED RIVER VALLEY

Objective: Playing at a steady pace, with no hesitation at changes from blow to draw on different holes. Emphases: 6 blow to 5 draw, 5 blow to 4 draw.

Before playing the entire song:
Practice the notes to the phrase, "hasten to bid me adieu," which ends with 6 blow to 5 draw to 5 blow to 4 draw. Practice the notes to the phrase, "And the one who has loved you so true," which ends with 5 blow to 4 draw to 5 blow to 4 draw to 4 blow.

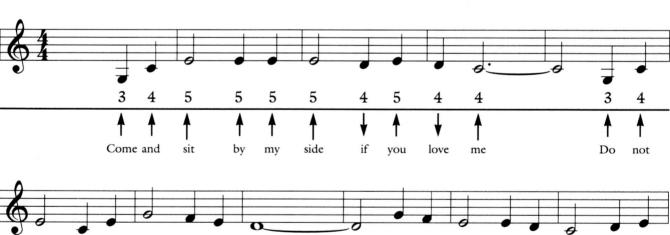

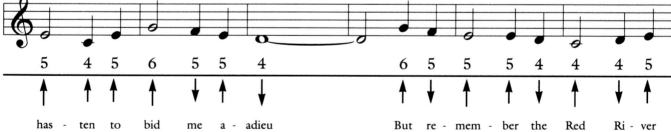

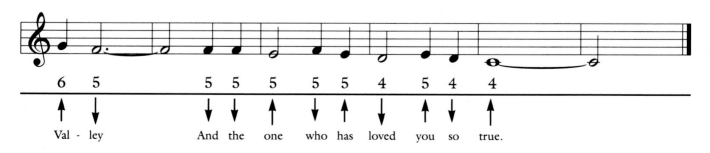

HEY LOLLY LOLLY

Objective:	Playing at a steady pace, with no hesitation at changes from blow to draw on different holes. Emphases: 6 blow to 5 draw, 5 blow to 4 draw.
Before playing the entire song:	
	Practice the notes to the last two measures, "Hey lolly lolly low," which ends with 6 blow to 5 draw to 5 blow to 4 draw to 4 blow.
Tip:	This is a pattern from "Red River Valley" that you've worked on, here with different phrasing.

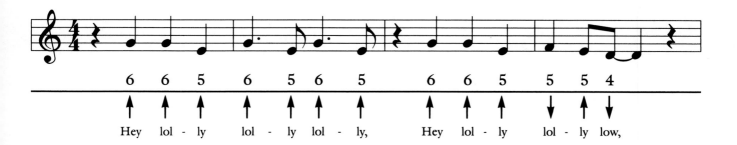

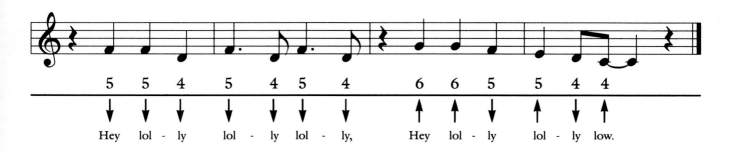

I KNOW WHERE I'M GOIN'

Objective: Playing at a steady pace, with no hesitation in skipping over holes.
Emphasis: 6 blow to 4 blow.

Before playing the entire song:
Practice the notes to the phrase, "I know who I love," which ends by
jumping from a 6 blow to a 4 blow.

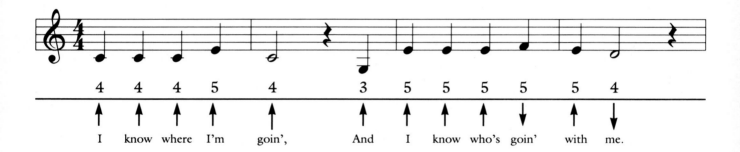

28

FAIR AND TENDER LADIES

Objective:	Playing at a steady pace, with no hesitation in moving between blow and draw notes on different holes. Emphases: 6 draw to 7 blow, 7 blow to 8 draw, 8 draw to 7 blow, and 7 blow to 6 draw.
Before playing the entire song:	Practice notes to the opening phrase, "Come all you fair and tender ladies," which includes all the emphases listed above.
Tip:	Play this as slowly as needed to keep a steady pace. Even at regular speed this is a slow song. Note the unusual way it ends, with an almost mournful sound.

Bringing in the Sheaves

Objective: Playing at a steady pace with no hesitation in moving between blow and draw notes on different holes. Emphases: 7 blow to 8 draw, 8 draw to 7 blow.

Before playing the entire song:
Practice the notes to the last two measures of the song, "We shall come rejoicing, Bringing in the sheaves," which focus on the movement between 8 draw and 7 blow.

by Knowles Shaw and George A. Minor

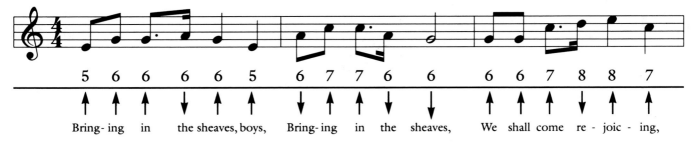

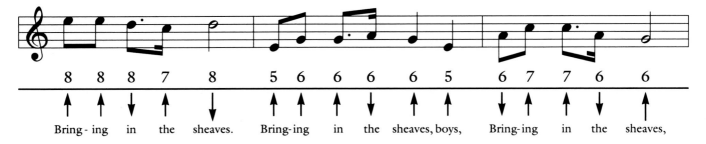

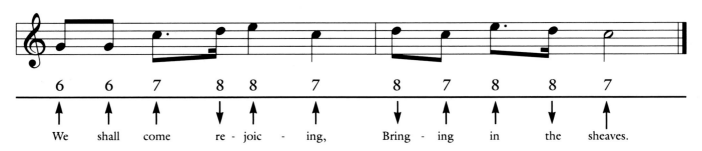

THE WATER IS WIDE

Objective:	Playing at a steady pace, with no hesitation in moving between blow and draw notes on different holes. Emphases: 7 blow to 8 draw, 8 draw to 7 blow, 7 blow to 6 draw, 6 blow to 7 draw, 8 blow to 9 draw, 9 draw to 8 blow.
Before playing the entire song:	Practice notes to the phrase, "And both shall row, my love and I," which includes many of the emphases listed above. Also practice the sequence 8 blow to 9 draw to 8 blow.
Tip:	Note that this song makes substantial use of the 8 and 9 holes. These reeds require very little air and can "choke" easily if they receive too much. If you need reassurance that the reeds work properly, hold the harmonica between your teeth around the area of these holes and breathe in and out.

IT'S A LONG LONG WAY TO TIPPERARY

Objective: Playing at a steady pace, with no hesitation in skipping over holes.
Emphasis: 9 draw to 6 draw.

Before playing the entire song:
Practice these two notes as they occur in the song with the word "Farewell."

by Jack Judge and Harry Williams

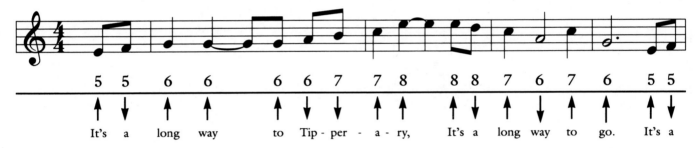

5 5 6 6 6 6 7 7 8 8 8 7 6 7 6 5 5

It's a long way to Tip - per - a - ry, It's a long way to go. It's a

6 6 6 6 7 7 8 8 8 8 6 7 7 8

long way to Tip - per - a - ry, To the sweet - est girl I know.

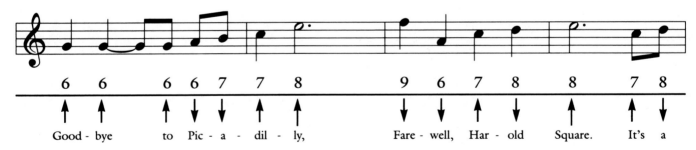

6 6 6 6 7 7 8 9 6 7 8 8 7 8

Good - bye to Pic - a - dil - ly, Fare - well, Har - old Square. It's a

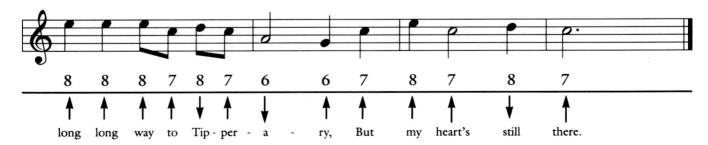

8 8 8 7 8 7 6 6 7 8 7 8 7

long long way to Tip - per - a - ry, But my heart's still there.

32

Spanish Is a Loving Tongue

Objective:	Achieving clear notes on holes that are not adjacent on the harmonica. Emphases: 4 blow to 7 blow, 7 blow to 5 blow.

Before playing the entire song:

Practice moving between these notes. There is a long pause between them in the song, giving you time to set up.

5	5	6	6	6	6	7	5	5	6	5
↑	↑	↑	↑	↓	↓	↑	↑	↑	↑	↑

Span - ish is a lov - ing tongue, Soft as mu - sic,
'Twas a girl I learned it from, Liv - ing down So -

1

4	4	4
↓	↑	↓

light as spray.

2

4	4	4	7	7	7	6	6	6	6	6	5	5	6	5
↓	↓	↑	↑	↑	↓	↑	↓	↓	↑	↑	↑	↑	↑	↑

no - ra way. I don't look much like a lo - ver, Yet I say her

4	4	5	4	5	5	6	6	6	6	7	5	5	6	5	4	4	4
↓	↑	↑	↓	↑	↑	↑	↓	↑	↓	↑	↑	↑	↑	↑	↓	↓	↑

love words o - ver Of - ten when I'm all a - lone: Mi a - mor, mi co - ra - zón.

OLD FOLKS AT HOME

Objective: Achieving clear notes on holes that are not adjacent on the harmonica within a phrase requiring movement from a draw note to a blow note on a different hole. Emphasis: 4 blow to 7 blow followed by 6 draw to 7 blow.

Before playing the entire song:
Practice these notes on the phrase "Swanee river."

by Stephen Foster

CHAPTER 4
Keys to Success

Now we come to the harmonica player's best-kept secret. Your harmonica is designed to play in the key of C. But you can play many other lovely songs in other keys. Many have beautiful, haunting melodies—melodies that *can't* be played on your harmonica in C. But playing them is easy. You'll need no skills beyond those you've already learned. If you can play clear single notes and can move smoothly from hole to hole, you can play songs in major keys such as F and G and minor keys such as D minor, E minor, and F minor.

This is possible for a simple reason. All the notes in the key of C are also notes in other keys. Some of your C harmonica's notes are part of the regular "do re mi" scale in those other keys, and some notes become "sharps" and "flats" (notes that are found in songs with richer melodies). These notes are readily available to you on your harmonica, played in the same way. The only difference is the relationship of the holes to each other. It will take some time to become familiar with this new dimension of your harmonica, especially if you've been playing "by ear."

The songs chosen for this next section are all in keys other than C. The objective here is to achieve a smooth flow of melody through practice. After a while, you'll be ready to surprise your friends with a whole slew of new songs in new keys!

(Key of D minor)

SINNER MAN

SHADY GROVE

(Key of D minor)

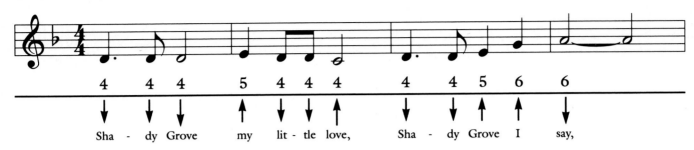

	4	4	4	5	4	4	4	4	4	5	6	6
	↓	↓	↓	↑	↓	↓	↑	↓	↓	↑	↑	↓
	Sha	-	dy Grove	my	lit	-	tle love,	Sha	-	dy Grove	I	say,

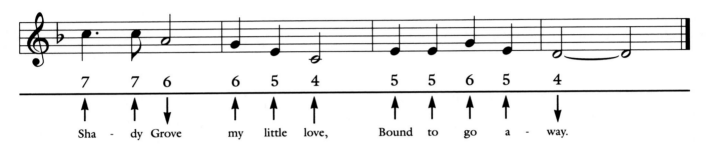

	7	7	6	6	5	4	5	5	6	5	4
	↑	↑	↓	↑	↑	↑	↑	↑	↑	↑	↓
	Sha	-	dy Grove	my	little	love,	Bound	to	go	a	- way.

DEEP BLUE SEA

(Key of G)

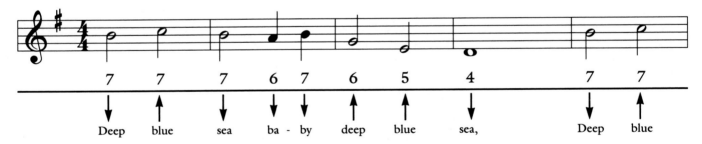

	7	7	7	6	7	6	5	4	7	7
	↓	↑	↓	↓	↓	↑	↑	↓	↓	↑
	Deep	blue	sea	ba	- by	deep	blue	sea,	Deep	blue

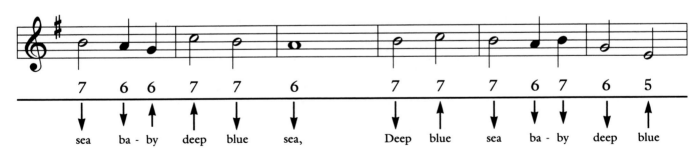

	7	6	6	7	7	6	7	7	7	6	7	6	5
	↓	↓	↑	↑	↓	↓	↓	↑	↓	↓	↓	↓	↑
	sea	ba	- by	deep	blue	sea,	Deep	blue	sea	ba	- by	deep	blue

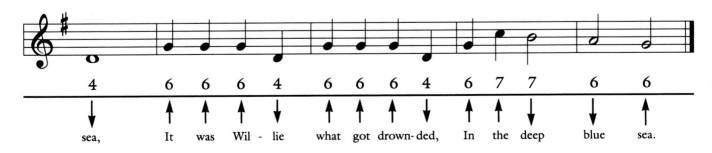

	4	6	6	6	4	6	6	6	4	6	7	7	6	6
	↓	↑	↑	↑	↓	↑	↑	↑	↓	↑	↑	↓	↓	↓
	sea,	It	was	Wil	- lie	what	got	drown- ded,	In	the	deep	blue		sea.

36

(Key of D minor)

SHABAT SHALOM

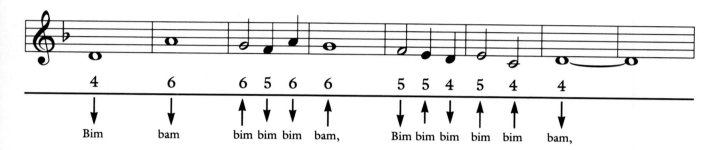

| 4 | 6 | 6 5 6 6 | 5 5 4 5 4 4 |

Bim bam bim bim bim bam, Bim bim bim bim bim bam,

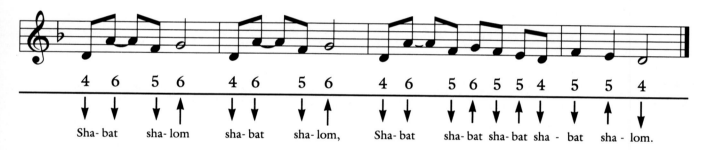

| 4 | 6 | 6 5 6 6 | 5 5 4 5 4 4 |

Bim bam bim bim bim bam, Bim bim bim bim bim bam,

| 4 6 5 6 | 4 6 5 6 | 4 6 5 6 5 5 4 5 5 4 |

Sha-bat sha-lom sha-bat sha-lom, Sha-bat sha-bat sha-bat sha-bat sha-lom.

(Key of E minor)

GROUND HOG

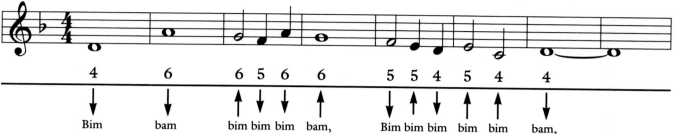

| 6 6 6 6 6 | 6 6 6 6 5 | 8 8 8 8 8 | 8 8 8 8 7 7 |

Get out your gun and whis-tle up your dog, Get out your gun and whis-tle up your dog, We're

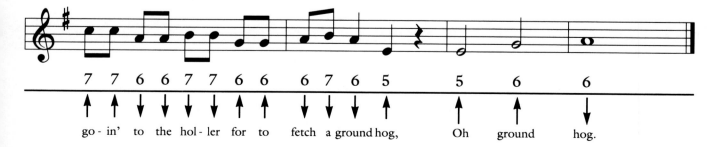

| 7 7 6 6 7 7 6 6 | 6 7 6 5 | 5 | 6 | 6 |

go-in' to the hol-ler for to fetch a ground hog, Oh ground hog.

WILL THE CIRCLE BE UNBROKEN

(Key of G)

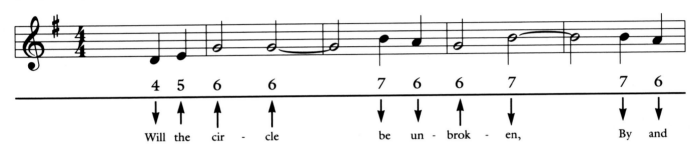

| 4 | 5 | 6 | 6 | 7 | 6 | 6 | 7 | 7 | 6 |
| Will | the | cir | - cle | be | un | - brok | - en, | By | and |

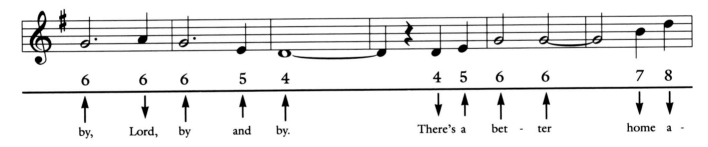

| 6 | 6 | 6 | 5 | 4 | 4 | 5 | 6 | 6 | 7 | 8 |
| by, | Lord, | by | and | by. | There's a | bet | - ter | home a - |

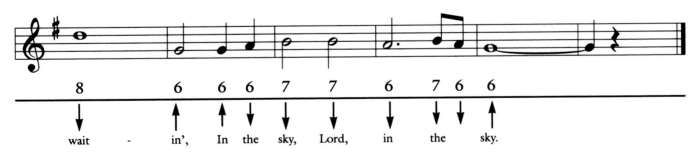

| 8 | 6 | 6 | 6 | 7 | 7 | 6 | 7 | 6 | 6 |
| wait | - in', | In | the | sky, | Lord, | in | the | sky. |

38

AWAY WITH RUM

(Key of F)

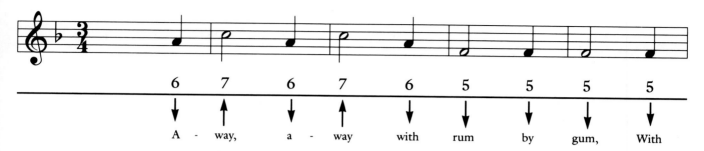

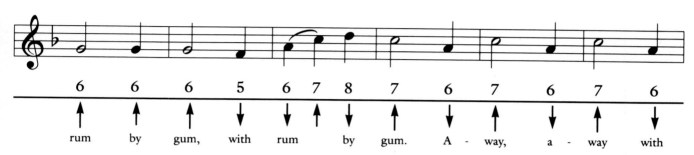

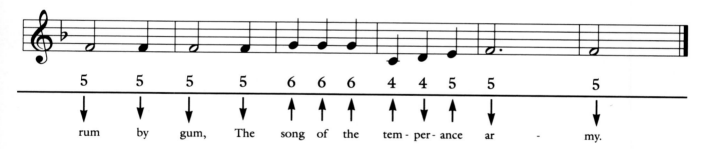

LEATHERWING BAT

(Key of E minor)

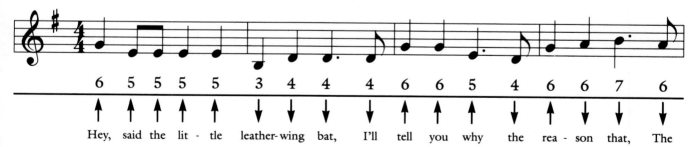

THE ERIE CANAL

(Key of D minor)

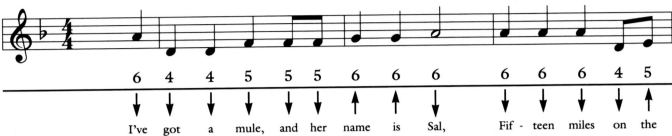

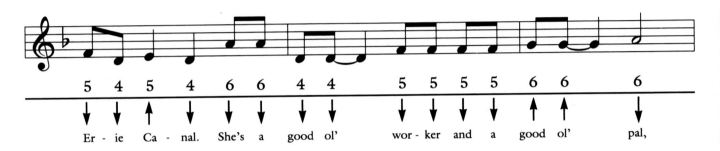

I've got a mule, and her name is Sal, Fif - teen miles on the

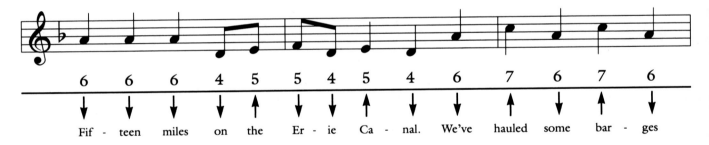

Er - ie Ca - nal. She's a good ol' wor - ker and a good ol' pal,

Fif - teen miles on the Er - ie Ca - nal. We've hauled some bar - ges

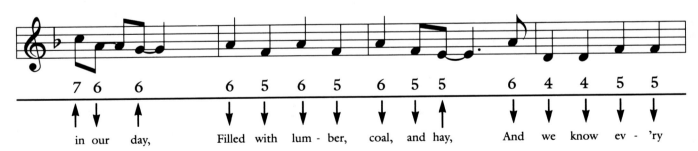

in our day, Filled with lum - ber, coal, and hay, And we know ev - 'ry

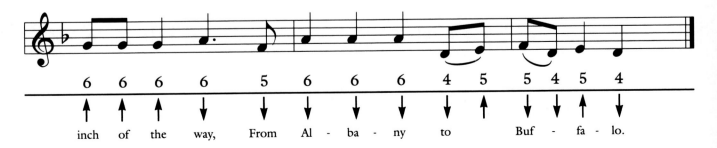

inch of the way, From Al - ba - ny to Buf - fa - lo.

CHAPTER 5
Impress Your Friends

You're at a party. The time comes for some entertainment, and the hosts remember that you play the harmonica. "How about a tune on the old mouth harp?" they say. This is *not* the time for Brahms' lullaby. But what do you play?

As it happens, there are a number of fancy-sounding songs that serve this purpose perfectly. These songs use two easy techniques: the "too-da-loo" and the "zip." Both techniques allow you to play notes quickly and smoothly, leaving your friends wondering where you learned such tricks.

The "too-da-loo" is just what it sounds like: nonsense syllables. Try saying these syllables without your harmonica: "too-da-loo." Say it, aloud, several times, emphasizing the "loo." Now try a longer phrase: "Too-da-loo, too-da-loo, too-da loo-loo-loo." This should sound familiar; it echoes the rhythmic pattern of a theme from the "William Tell Overture." That overture was used in radio and television versions of *The Lone Ranger*. If you remember that theme, try singing it using "too-da-loo, too-da-loo, too-da-loo-loo-loo." As you do this, think about how you are using your tongue to enunciate the "too-da-loos."

You can play this theme on your harmonica by playing the notes shown in the music. But, instead of blowing or drawing each separate note, use your tongue (tongue only, not your voice) to enunciate the "too-da-loo" syllables behind the note. Enunciating "too-da-loo" provides a preprogrammed rhythm, so the notes flow easily. You can also use this technique—with variations in the syllables used—with other songs in this section.

The "zip" is even easier. Again, the word says it all. To do the "zip," just start blowing at the bottom of your harmonica (that is, near the 1 and 2 holes). As you blow, slide the harmonica across your mouth quickly and without stopping, all the way to the top: "zip"! Chico Marx did this on the piano when he would run his thumb up the keys, sounding each note. This works even better on a harmonica. This technique can be used in a number of ways. For example, you can add this to the end of most songs in the key of C when you want to add a "flourish."

WILLIAM TELL OVERTURE

Objective:	To play long sequences of the same note in a smooth, flowing manner. Emphases: 6 blow, 7 draw and blow, 8 draw and blow.
Before playing the entire song:	Check your clear single notes on holes 6 and above. Remember, you need very little air to sound these holes. Sing the song through using "too-da-loos."
Tip:	If it's easier, you can use an "oo" sound instead of a "loo" sound.

by Antonio Rossini

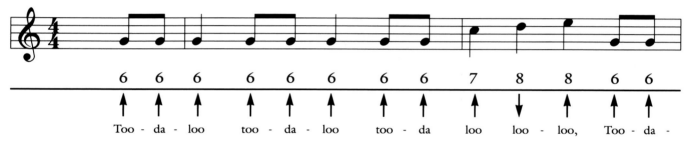

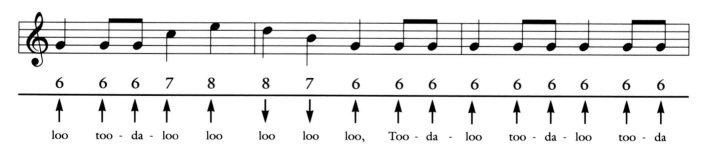

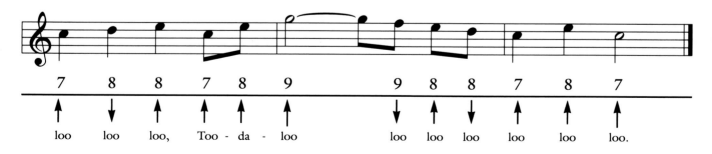

WHAT SHALL WE DO WITH A DRUNKEN SAILOR

Objective:	To play long sequences of the same note in a smooth, flowing manner. Emphases: holes 6 to 8, blow and draw.
Before playing the entire song:	Sing the song through using "too-da-loos" instead of the words.
Tip:	The syllables only need to mirror the rhythm and flow of the words; any syllables that do this will work.

(Key of F)

CRIPPLE CREEK (CHORUS)

Objective: To play long sequences of the same note in a smooth, flowing manner, including a "zip" ending.

Before playing the entire song:
Sing the song through using "too-da-loos" instead of the words. On the last note, blow into the harmonica and slide upward, off the end of it. This is the "zip." Though it is marked using holes 7 through 10, you can start right on your ending note, C.

Tip: The "zip" can also be used to lead into the verse of this song; see page 41. To add this "zip," first practice blowing while you slide up from the 1 hole to the 5 hole. When you are able to stop at the 5 hole, you can start the song by zipping to the 5 blow, which begins the song. In musical terms, this technique is known as a "glissando."

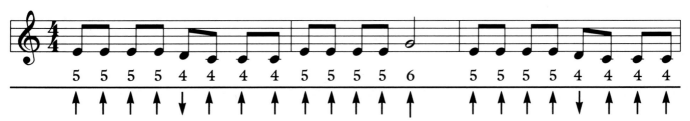

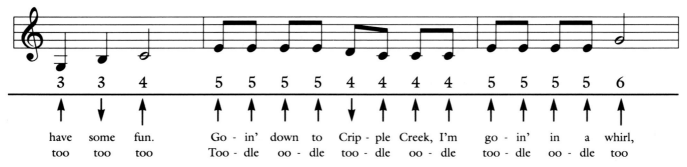

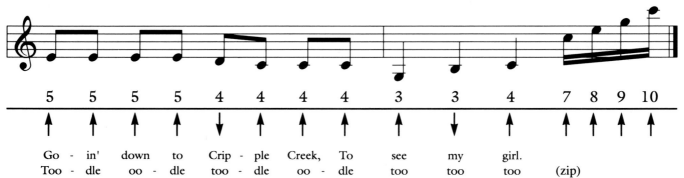

CHAPTER 6
Using Simple Chords

A chord is two or more notes played at the same time. Using simple chords can add fullness and harmony to your playing. And as with almost everything else on the harmonica, chords are easy to find.

Often, when trying to blow a single hole, you may blow two holes. When you do so, you are playing a simple chord. The effect can be quite pretty. In fact (as you may already have discovered), many songs in this book can be played most of the way through using two holes rather than one.

The melody of "Skip to My Lou," for example, begins on the 5 hole blow. But you can blow *both* the 5 and the 4 holes to start. For every note in the melody, in fact, you can play both the hole shown and the hole under it. That's an example of using simple chords. Many of the songs in this book have been chosen because they can be played using simple chords. If playing two notes does not sound "right" at any point, simply play the single note instead. By experimenting using chords and single notes, you should be able to find chords for most songs.

You may also want to use fuller chords. Because of the unique design of the harmonica, a full C chord exists on any three adjacent blow notes. Songs in C normally end with a note in the C chord; as a result, instead of ending on a single note, you can end with that note and the notes around it, giving your song a chord ending. For songs in the key of G, you can get a G chord by drawing on holes 1 through 4.

SWING LOW, SWEET CHARIOT

Objective: To use simple chords to improve the effect of this song.

Before playing the entire song:

Try the chord made up of holes 1 through 3 blow (a C chord), followed by the chord made by holes 1 and 2 draw (a G chord).

Tip: Make sure the harmonica is far enough in your mouth and that you are drawing lightly on the holes. Too much air can make the 2 draw go flat. Notice that the 2 draw and 3 blow are the same note (G). The music for this song is written using the 3 blow, but it is excellent practice to use the 2 draw whenever possible.

(Key of G)

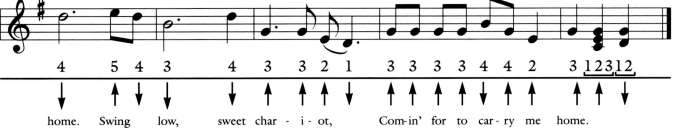

46

NOBODY KNOWS THE TROUBLE I'VE SEEN

Objective:	To use simple chords to improve the effect of this song.
Before playing the entire song:	
	Try the chord made up of holes 6 and 7 blow, followed by the chord made by holes 5 and 6 draw.
Tip:	Except for the final chords, this song can also be played in the key of C starting on the 8 blow or in the key of G starting on the 7 draw. If you want to play by ear, finding the holes used to play this song in those keys will be good practice.

(Key of F)

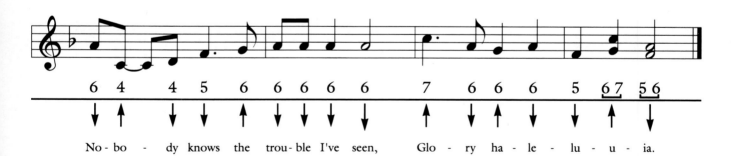

47

OH SUSANNA

Objective:	To use simple chords to improve the effect of this song.
Before playing the entire song:	
	Try blowing and drawing holes 5 and 6. Try blowing holes 3, 4, and 5, then drawing holes 1, 2, 3, and 4, then blowing holes 1, 2, 3, and 4.
Tip:	The version shown here uses chords sparingly. But, except in one or two places—especially the "oh" in "Oh Susannah"—the song can be played using the single hole and the hole below it.

by Stephen Foster

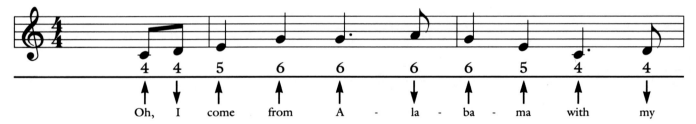

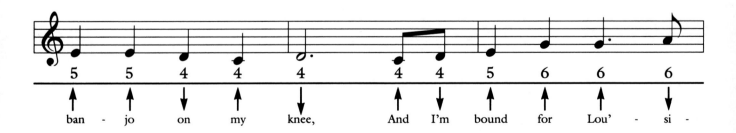

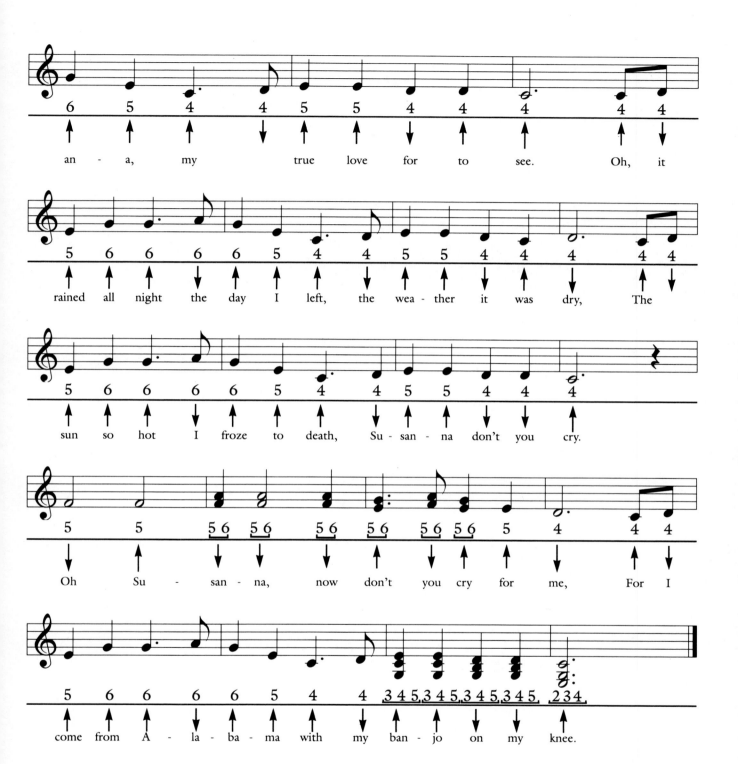

JACOB'S LADDER

Problem:	While having a pretty melody, "Jacob's Ladder" is almost always presented in harmony. How can this effect be achieved on the harmonica?
Tip:	Experiment with using the melody note shown and sometimes adding the hole below it.

CHAPTER 7
Building Your Skills

This section provides opportunities to test your skills. Each song requires a somewhat different approach and presents special challenges. We'll offer some tips for addressing those problems. Spend some time looking at each song before playing it. After you have worked on it for a while, consider taping yourself on a small tape recorder and listening to how you sound. This is one of the best ways to improve your playing.

(Key of G)

BOOGIE

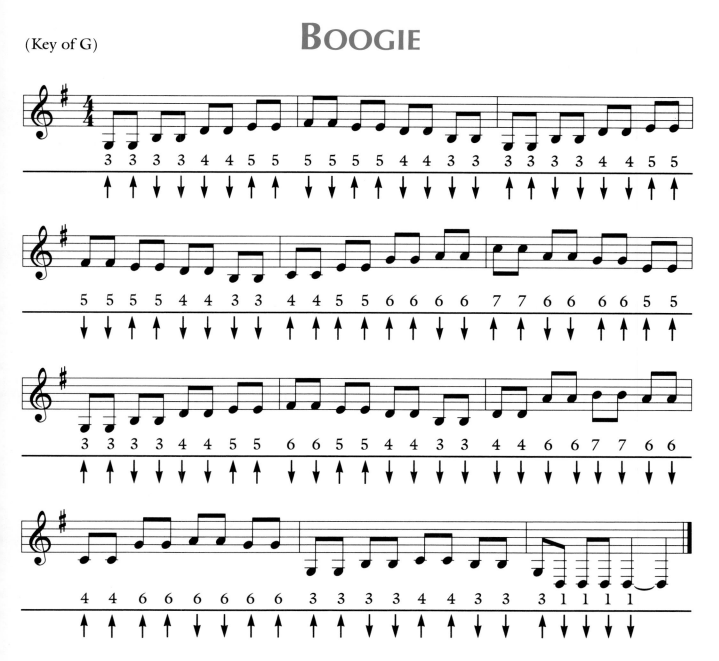

ODE TO JOY

Problem:	"Ode to Joy," from the fourth movement of Beethoven's Ninth Symphony, has many notes: Each measure has three or four notes. In playing it, the melody must *flow*.
Tip:	Try to keep a steady flow of air, so that the harmonica's reeds are always sounding. Don't think of the notes as separate but as each flowing into the next.

by Ludwig van Beethoven

52

FRANKIE AND JOHNNY

Problem:	This classic blues tune includes a seven-note passage that goes back and forth between blow and draw on different notes. To play this song well, this passage must be played smoothly. How can smooth playing of a long, complicated passage be developed?
Tip:	Break the passage into two-note sequences and practice each sequence separately. Next try three-note sequences, then four-note sequences, and so on, until you are playing the entire seven-note sequence.

SKYE BOAT SONG

Problem:	More than half of this beautiful Scottish melody consists of draw notes, so playing it quickly fills up the lungs. How can air intake be controlled on such a song?
Tip:	For songs in the key of G it is usually best to start playing with your lungs almost empty. Then use the blow notes to exhale some air. It takes practice to determine the appropriate breathing pattern on an individual song.

(Key of G)

by Annie McLeod and Sir Henry R. Bishop

54

ROSIN THE BEAU

Problem:	This enjoyable song is pitched high. What can be done to bring it down to the lower ranges of the harmonica?
Tip:	"Rosin the Beau" can be played in the key of F by starting on the 4 hole blow rather than the 4 hole draw and then picking out the right notes. It can also be played in C starting on the 3 hole blow, but one of the notes requires "note bending." Another alternative is to buy a harmonica in a lower key.

(Key of G)

55

CHAPTER 8
Repertoire

Whether you're sitting under a blue sky on a wooded hillside or you're plunked down at the kitchen table after dinner, there is no better musical friend than a little harmonica. You can express feelings, tell a story, or just relax with your favorite songs.

We've brought together some popular melodies that you're now ready to play. You've practiced movements between holes, and you know how to enunciate syllables behind your notes. Your hands should be curling around your harmonica to shape the sound and to add vibrato. If you've followed this far, you'll find nothing in these songs that you haven't already practiced. This repertoire collection begins with some longtime American favorites and then moves into children's and holiday songs. A good rule: Start with songs you know well and enjoy the most!

If you haven't attempted to pick out a song "by ear," this is a good place to try. Quite simply, the more you play your harmonica in this manner, the more you will learn. An easy way to start playing by ear is to choose a song in this section that you know well enough to hum. Turn to that page and look *only* at the starting hole—then close the book. Try finding the second, then the third and fourth notes, and so on. You may get more wrong notes than right ones at first, but you'll be surprised how quickly you learn. When you're done, play the song again.

As you play more, from the book or by ear, your skills will grow almost by themselves. Our goal is to give you the pleasure of "music in your pocket." It's a pleasure that can last a lifetime.

When the Saints Go Marching In

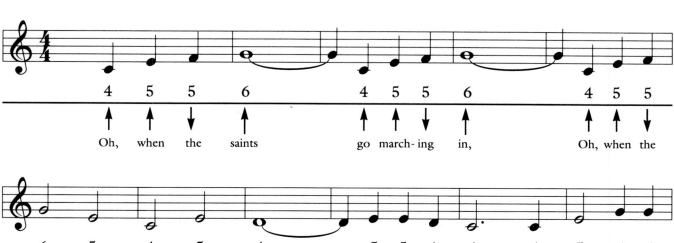

Oh, when the saints go march-ing in, Oh, when the

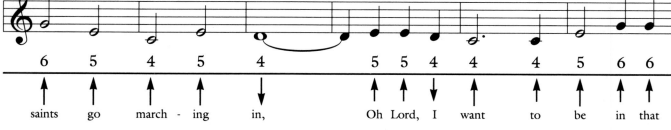

saints go march - ing in, Oh Lord, I want to be in that

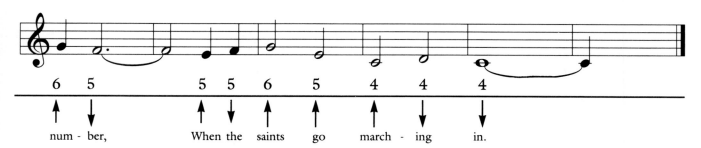

num - ber, When the saints go march - ing in.

AMAZING GRACE

(Key of G)

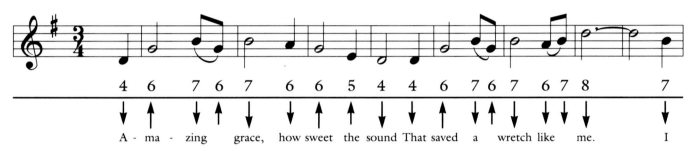

4   6   7 6   7   6   6   5   4   4   6   7 6   7   6 7   8   7

A - ma - zing   grace, how sweet the sound That saved   a   wretch like   me.   I

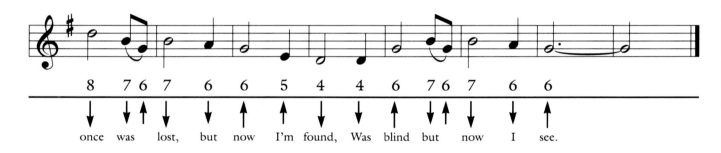

8   7 6   7   6   6   5   4   4   6   7 6   7   6   6

once was   lost,   but   now   I'm found,   Was   blind but   now   I   see.

WHEN JOHNNY COMES MARCHING HOME

(Key of A minor)

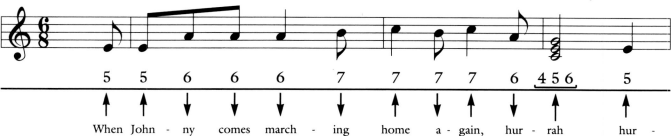

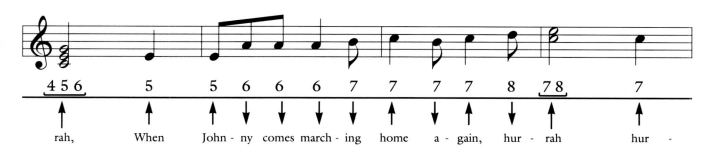

When John - ny comes march - ing home a - gain, hur - rah hur -

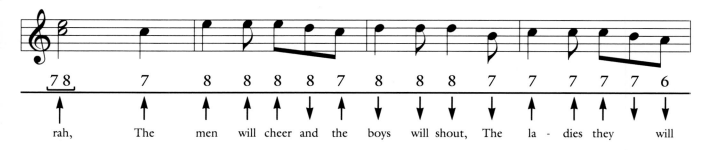

rah, When John - ny comes march - ing home a - gain, hur - rah hur -

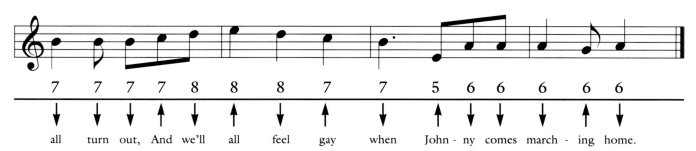

rah, The men will cheer and the boys will shout, The la - dies they will

all turn out, And we'll all feel gay when John - ny comes march - ing home.

DIXIE

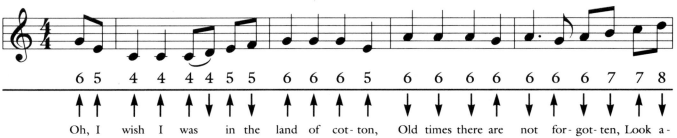

6 5   4   4   4 4 5 5   6 6 6 5   6 6   6 6   6 6   6 7   7 8

↑↑ ↑ ↑ ↑ ↑↑↑↑ ↑↑↑↑ ↓ ↓ ↓↑ ↓↑ ↓ ↓↓

Oh, I wish I was in the land of cot-ton, Old times there are not for-got-ten, Look a-

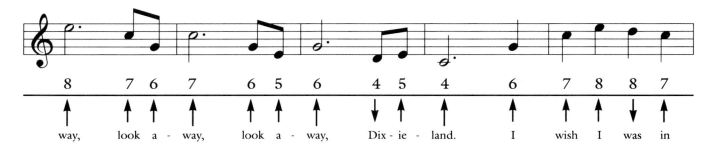

8   7 6   7   6 5   6   4 5   4   6   7 8 8 7

↑ ↑ ↑ ↑ ↑ ↑ ↑ ↓ ↑ ↑ ↑ ↑ ↑ ↓ ↑

way,   look a - way,   look a - way,   Dix - ie - land.   I   wish I was in

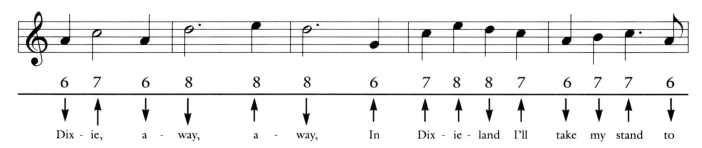

6   7   6   8   8   8   6   7 8 8 7   6 7 7   6

↓ ↑ ↓ ↓ ↑ ↓ ↑ ↑↓↑↑ ↓↓↑ ↓

Dix - ie,   a - way,   a - way,   In   Dix - ie - land I'll take my stand to

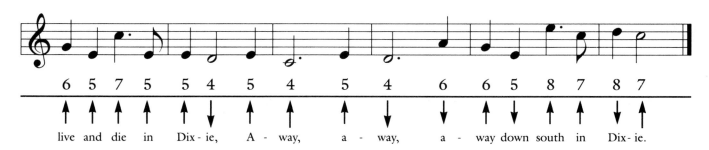

6 5 7 5   5 4   5   4   5   4   6   6 5   8 7   8 7

↑↑↑↑ ↑↓ ↑ ↓ ↑ ↓ ↓ ↑↓ ↑↑ ↓↑

live and die in Dix - ie, A - way,   a - way,   a - way down south in Dix - ie.

THE YELLOW ROSE OF TEXAS

OLD MACDONALD HAD A FARM

LONDON BRIDGE

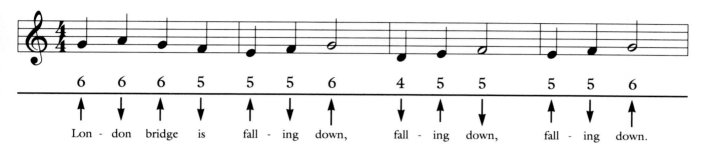

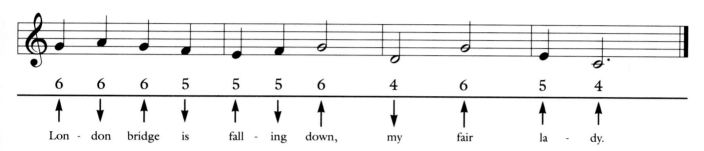

AWAY IN A MANGER

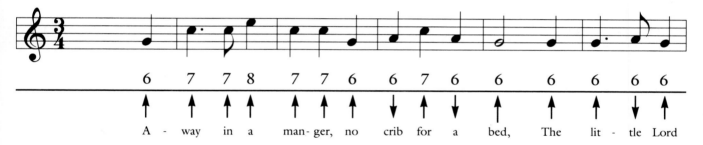

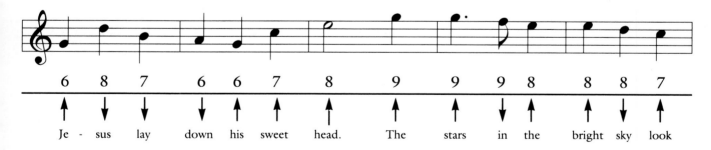

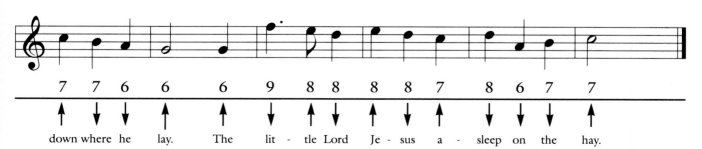

JOY TO THE WORLD

64